POP ACADEMY

From Grit to Global Impact: The Inspiring Journey of Vishnu

Transforming Lives Through Community Empowerment and Climate Action

Author
Dr. Ash Pachauri

Contributors
Dr. Saroj Pachauri
Manish Gupta

Cover Design
Manish Gupta

First edition

This book was professionally typeset on Reedsy.
Find out more at reedsy.com

Contents

A Personal Message

Dear Readers,

Thank you for taking the time to explore my journey. My story is one of resilience, perseverance, and unwavering hope. It's a testament to the power of community, the incredible work we accomplished when we're together, and the profound impact each of us can have when we commit to making a difference.

From the bustling lanes of Sanjay Gandhi Transport Nagar to the global stage, every step of my journey has been fueled by the love and support of those around me. The loss of my father and adoptive parents, the separation from my beloved wife during the pandemic, and the devastating effects of climate change were all challenges that tested my resolve. Yet, these experiences also strengthened my determination to create a better world for my family and community.

Our work on self-care interventions, community empowerment, and climate action has shown that positive change is possible, even in the face of adversity. The visuals we created, which gained recognition from the World Health Organization, are a testament to the collective effort and dedication of everyone involved.

To the young leaders and changemakers reading this, I want you to know that your dreams are within reach. Embrace the challenges, learn from them, and never lose sight of your vision. Surround yourself with those who believe in you, and let their support guide you through difficult times.

Together, we can build a more sustainable, equitable, and compassionate world. Thank you for being a part of this journey and for your commitment to making a difference. Remember, no matter where you start, your impact can be boundless.

With gratitude and hope,

Manish Gupta

The Early Days

Young Manish Gupta also known affectionately as Vishnu was born on July 12, 1990 in Bhidhuna, Auraiya District, Uttar Pradesh, India. At the young age of 14, he moved to the heart of Sanjay Gandhi Transport Nagar, Asia's largest trucking halt point, where trucks rumbled and honked through the narrow lanes of truck loading and offloading locations, storage units, warehouses, and allied businesses (mechanical workshops, industrial tire and part outlets, and tea stalls, locally known as *dhabas*). The dense air was filled with the mingling scents of diesel, food, and sweat. This was North India's prime truck stop, a bustling hive of activity that never slept. For Vishnu, it was home.

On the peripheries of the sprawling 77 acres of Sanjay Gandhi Transport Nagar, Vishnu witnessed a harsh and troubling reality as it unfolded. Among the discarded items that litter the area were used needles, a stark reminder of the pervasive drug use. Women and transgender sex workers could be seen soliciting, as they navigate a precarious existence in this bustling transport hub. The surrounding parks, bushes, and even the trucks themselves became sites of illicit sex, casting a shadow over the lives of those who frequent the area. This hidden side of the transport hub underscored the pressing need for comprehensive support and intervention to address the complex challenges faced by this marginalized community.

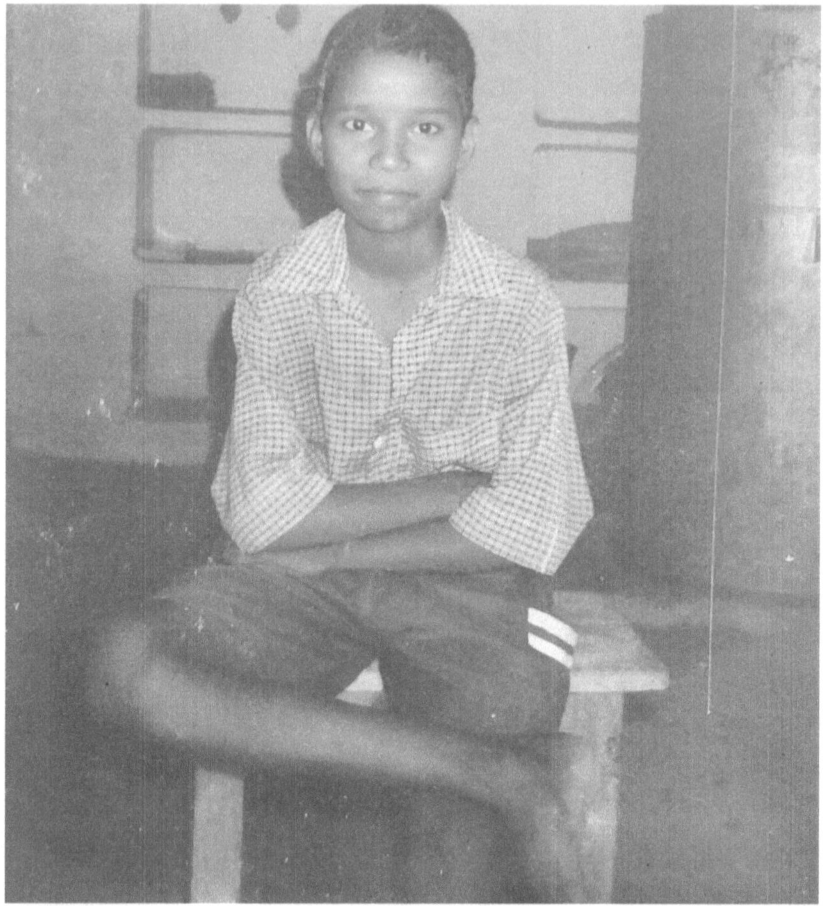

Vishnu at 8 Years

Vishnu's uncle, Radhey Shyam Gupta and his wife, Iccha Devi, his local guardians and beloved, adoptive parents, ran a small tea stall at Sanjay Gandhi Transport Nagar that catered to the endless stream of truck drivers and their helpers. Life in the transport hub was a daily grind, and Vishnu worked multiple jobs, including helping on trucking routes, to make ends meet.

When he returned to the truck stop, sometimes after months enroute highways, Vishnu ran errands, delivered tea to the drivers, and assisted his uncle at the tea stall. He learned to navigate the chaotic environment, his small frame darting between trucks and people easily. These interactions with the drivers opened his eyes to the hardships they endured—long hours on the road, poor living conditions, and health issues from prolonged driving and exposure to pollutants.

Despite the noise and chaos, Vishnu had a curious mind and a thirst for knowledge. Though not formally educated, his parents valued learning and ensured he attended the local school. Economic pressures forced him to drop out of school. Still, his limited reading and writing skills made it possible for him to volunteer with local NGOs and community-based organizations in his area.

A Fortuitous Introduction

Vishnu's journey took a transformative turn when his sharp and shrewd cousin, a community leader, introduced him to who would become his lifetime mentor, Dr. Ash Pachauri. Dr. Pachauri, then Director of the Center for Human Progress (www.thechp.org), was renowned for his work and influence. When an in-person meeting was finally set up in a local park, Vishnu expected to meet a mature, formal official. Instead, he was stunned to encounter a young man dressed in shorts and riding a bicycle. Dr. Pachauri's casual and approachable disposition immediately put Vishnu at ease.

Despite having no prior experience with community work, lacking knowledge in reading, writing, and even speaking in a professional context, and never having used a computer or email, Vishnu was determined to make an impression. With heartfelt sincerity, he convinced Dr. Pachauri that he was the right person to hire as a volunteer for community projects at the Center for Human Progress. His passion, willingness to learn, and deep understanding of the local community resonated with Dr. Pachauri, who saw potential in Vishu's raw determination. This unexpected encounter marked the beginning of a profound mentorship and friendship, shaping Vishnu's future endeavors and solidifying his path in community empowerment and climate action.

Unsurprisingly, given Vishnu's grit and determination to learn, he excelled in community work with the Center for Human Progress where he learned about community-based approaches to participatory community-led communication, including Magnet Theater and Interpersonal Communication tools (see below).

Discovering a Passion for Photography

It was through his community work that Vishnu discovered a love for photography. Dr. Pachauri, having recently been introduced to renowned Nat Geo photographer Mahesh Nair (read more about Mahesh Nair here: https://www.imagesnbeyond.com/about), recognized Vishnu's potential and passion. Deeply committed to sharing his gift, Mr. Nair generously offered to train Vishnu. Through the Center for Human Progress, Vishnu received invaluable training in photography, honing his skills under the guidance of a master. Encouraged by his peers and inspired by his mentor, Vishnu's journey transcended the confines of his beginnings, opening up new horizons and opportunities.

Vishnu with Mahesh Nair

Community Training in Photography with Vishnu and Mahesh Nair

Inspired by the transformative power of photography, Vishnu realized he could use this medium to empower his community. He began training local members, teaching them to use photography as a tool for community expression and empowerment. His peers, seeing his potential, played a crucial role in his journey, encouraging him to dream beyond the confines of the tea stall.

Magnet Theater is an intervention designed to not only entertain and educate, but to involve audience members in the action and encourage the kind of participation and reflection that is key to sustained behavior change. It is a form of dialogue-based, participatory theater led by- and for- communities that typically takes place in outdoor, public spaces, local and natural to the community. The hour-long performances explore issues affecting a community and encourage discussion and problem solving with audience members. The actors perform a drama that presents a dilemma based on community issues. The audience participates by offering suggestions to the characters or by taking the place of an actor and acting out solutions to the dilemma. Magnet Theater encourages audience members to discuss solutions and allows them to experiment in a safe environment, to encourage individual and community-wide change. Magnet Theater is different from other forms of community theater because it targets and attracts specific and repeat audiences, takes place at a regular time at a given venue, which local to the community, and serves as a forum for magnification of behavior change. The audience itself becomes the actor as it critically thinks about and analyzes solutions playing them out in 'real-world' scenarios through theater performances. Read more about Magnet Theater here: https://www. path.org/ (InterAct Project).

Vishnu in a Magnet Theater Performance

Vishnu at a Magnet Theater Performance with Props (Dressed as a Cop)

Vishnu in Various Magnet Theater Performances

Interpersonal Communication tools help move beyond message giving to face-to-face interaction, dialogue, and critical reflection led by- and for-communities, helping them to identify and analyze barriers to health and risk reduction, and plan ways to address them. Interpersonal communication as a behavior change intervention moves from one-way message giving to instead focus on processes involving community dialogue and discussion about local contexts and barriers to risk reduction, care, and treatment. Read more about Interpersonal Communication tools here: https://www.path.org/ (InterAct Project).

Vishnu Conducting Interpersonal Communication with Drivers at Sanjay Gandhi Transport Nagar

Vishnu Training Truck Drivers and Helpers in Uttar Pradesh, India

A Glimpse of Possibilities

Vishnu's creative prowess earned him a full-time role at the prestigious Center for Human Progress, a unique opportunity for someone from his background. Leaving behind the familiar streets of Sanjay Gandhi Transport Nagar, Vishnu stepped into a world he had only heard about in stories and books. While the work he led now was a stark contrast to the gritty environment of his childhood, he continued living at the trucking halt point and working with his peers to create capacities for them to promote health, wellness, and self-care.

Adjusting to this new world was not easy. Vishnu worked hard to understand the key principles of community-led participatory approaches to communication and interventions, principles of community leadership, and empowerment. His determination kept him focused on work and training while he continued his educational aspirations to become a qualified social worker. He also trained in climate action and community-based health programs and interventions; driven by his desire to address the issues he had seen firsthand. The more he learned, the more he understood the deep connections between environmental factors and public health.

Action and Advocacy

Vishnu threw himself into his work, often spending long hours in the field talking to his peers and allied communities, including sex workers and drug users. His hard work paid off, and he earned the respect of his community, colleagues, and peers as he developed the skills to become a master trainer in community-based methodologies and empowerment. He also became involved in various field activities, engaging his peers in photography training, sustainability and health skills, and advocacy training.

Eager to elevate the advocacy efforts of his community, Vishnu seized the opportunity to enhance his skills by enrolling in a documentary filmmaking program offered at a nominal cost by an NGO in southern India. Supported by the Center for Human Progress, this technical training empowered him to advance advocacy for his own community and beyond. He applied his newfound photography and filming skills to document and participate in clean-up drives, awareness campaigns, and community-led research projects. Vishnu was always eager to apply his knowledge to real-world problems, using his talents to drive meaningful change.

Discovering a Calling

During his first year at the Center for Human Progress, an NGO renowned for its community empowerment work, Vishnu embarked on a journey that would forever change his life. He participated in national and international events, engaging with government officials and UN diplomats. This invaluable exposure highlighted the critical importance of amplifying voices for advocacy and broadened his understanding of environmental degradation and public health crises.

The experience was profoundly transformative. Vishnu traveled across the country, tirelessly working with communities affected by HIV, human rights violations, inadequate sanitation, and the physical and mental toll of extreme pollution. As he witnessed firsthand the struggles and resilience of those he served, his commitment to making a difference deepened, solidifying his resolve to advocate for change on a global scale.

Vishnu at the Airport on his First Trip by Plane

Vishnu's First Time on an Aircraft (With His Team)

One striking example of his grit and dedication occurred just days after joining the Center for Human Progress. Vishnu persuaded his mentor to allow him to volunteer as a photographer on a project that took him to a city grappling with the nutritional needs and human rights of HIV-positive women, gay, and transgender sex workers. This opportunity led Vishnu on his first-ever airplane ride to Mysore in southern India.

In Mysore, he witnessed a community suffering from severe human rights abuses and health issues due to their social, sexual, and immunocompromised status. Vishnu and his team worked tirelessly to engage and empower these communities by mobilizing, educating, and training them on community organization, health and hygiene practices, and human rights advocacy. This hands-on experience reinforced his unwavering commitment to making a difference, leaving an indelible mark on his heart and driving his passion for global advocacy.

Vishnu Conducting Dialogue with Truck Drivers

Vishnu Sharing Health Information with the Community

Vishnu Counseling a Truck Driver

Visit some of Vishu's community-led, advocacy projects, including the Mysore project here.

Positive Habba, Mysore: http://www.thechp.org/projects-3.html

Project 19: http://www.thechp.org/projects.html

Knowledge FAN: http://www.thechp.org/knowledge-fan.html

My Voice: http://www.thechp.org/my-voice.html

Vishnu in Mysore, India

Bonding Through the POP Movement

After gaining extensive experience with the Center for Human Progress, a few years later, Vishnu was offered a full-time position with the POP (Protect Our Planet) Movement (www.thepopmovement.org), a global initiative dedicated to inspiring climate action among youth. The movement's mission aligned perfectly with his aspirations, and he eagerly accepted the role. As a young leader within the organization, Vishnu brought a unique perspective shaped by his experiences in Sanjay Gandhi Transport Nagar and his work with the Center for Human Progress. At the POP Movement, Vishnu went on to work very closely with Dr. R.K. Pachauri, who became key mentor to him. Under Dr. Pachauri's mentorship, Vishnu gained deep insights into climate action and sustainable development. This relationship was transformative, providing him with guidance, support, and a sense of belonging that profoundly shaped his personal and professional journey.

Through the POP Movement, Vishnu's relationship with Dr. R.K. Pachauri deepened significantly. He spent extensive time with Dr. Pachauri, traveling with him to various conferences, workshops, and community engagements. These travels were not just professional excursions; they were opportunities for Vishnu to learn directly from a seasoned leader in climate action. Dr. Pachauri imparted invaluable knowledge and insights, shaping Vishnu's understanding of environmental advocacy.

Vishnu's relationship with the Pachauri family blossomed into one of profound and meaningful connection. He became a treasured member of the family, supporting them as a friend and family member through both their most celebratory moments and extreme challenges. Through this bond, Vishnu learned invaluable lessons about friendship, family bonds, and professional dedication.

He went on to be mentored by Dr. R.K. Pachauri, who guided him in the field of climate action, and Dr. Saroj Pachauri, who provided deep insights into public health issues. These mentorships became the pillars of Vishnu's mission, shaping his life's work and becoming his *raison d'être*. Their guidance and support were instrumental in his journey, as he strived to make a lasting impact on the world through climate advocacy and public health initiatives.

Vishnu, Dr. R.K. Pachauri, and the POP family

Vishnu even lived in the Pachauri household for extended periods, where he was embraced as a family member. This close-knit environment allowed him to support Dr. Pachauri in numerous ways, particularly in film, photography, and outreach activities for climate action. Vishnu's skills in visual storytelling became instrumental in documenting the movement's initiatives and spreading its message to a broader audience.

Their bond was strengthened further by shared passions outside of work. Both avid cricket fans and players, Vishnu and Dr. Pachauri often took breaks to enjoy a match together. Whether watching a live game or reruns on TV, these moments of leisure were cherished. They not only provided a much-needed respite from their demanding work but also fostered a deeper personal connection between mentor and mentee.

These experiences were formative for Vishnu, blending professional growth with personal enrichment. Through his time with Dr. Pachauri, Vishnu gained not only a mentor but also a father figure, solidifying his commitment to climate action and strengthening his resolve to make a difference in the world.

Making a Mark

Vishnu's early projects with the POP Movement focused on grassroots initiatives. He worked closely with communities, educating them about sustainable practices and the importance of environmental conservation. He traveled to urban slums and industrial areas, always emphasizing the need for collective action. With his initiative, the POP Movement expanded its outreach. Vishnu spearheaded several educational programs among the neediest communities, including those focused on clean drinking water initiatives, sanitation, and climate change and health educational programs. His ability to connect with people from diverse backgrounds made him a natural leader and an effective advocate.

One of the notable projects contributed to by Vishnu was organized in Mexico in 2019 (read more: https://thepopmovement.org/event/international-conference-pop-festival-for-youth-led-climate-action/). At the International Conference & POP Festival which brought together several young climate leaders from around the world, Vishnu supported Latin American indigenous communities to amplify their voices regarding solar-powered technologies and water purification systems to benefit indigenous communities in rural areas. These systems, designed by indigenous communities, provided clean drinking water and reduced reliance on fossil fuels, promoting environmental sustainability. The success of this project garnered significant media attention, bringing Vishnu's multimedia, film, and photography talents into the spotlight. He became a rising star in the field of environmental film, photography, and creative work.

Vishnu at the POP Festival 2019, Mexico

Vishnu in Mexico

Vishnu with the POP Family in Mexico, 2019

Read more about POP Movement's Festivals here: https://thepopmovement.org/pop_festival/

Learn More About the POP Festival Here:
https://www.youtube.com/watch?v=XvsN7Dph4vM&t=7s

Thank you for accompanying me on this journey so far. Your support and interest in my story mean the world to me and the communities I strive to uplift. As you continue to read, I hope you find inspiration and hope in the pages ahead.

I kindly ask you to share your honest review of this book. Your feedback is invaluable and can help spread our message further, allowing us to reach more hearts and minds. By sharing your thoughts, you support not just me but also the countless communities working towards a brighter, more sustainable future.

Together, we can make a lasting impact.

With gratitude,

Vishnu

Community Empowerment

Vishnu's work in participatory community-led communication and empowerment, which he is now applying to community work worldwide, was deeply influenced by his time at the Center for Human Progress. He understood that sustainable change required more than just infrastructure; it required building the capacity of community members themselves. Vishnu's deep appreciation for this began with his unique experience in capturing Shanti Devi's story, which went viral and spread worldwide.

The Story of Shanti Devi: A Trailblazer in a Man's World

A unique story was unfolding in Sanjay Gandhi Transport Nagar amidst the cacophony of engines and the endless stream of trucks. Shanti Devi, the only woman truck mechanic in the area, had become a local legend. Her journey, marked by resilience and determination, symbolized community empowerment and gender equality.

Shanti Devi's life had not been easy. Born into a family of laborers, she had been forced to drop out of school at a young age to support her family. Her husband, an alcoholic, had passed away in an accident, leaving her to fend for herself. In a community where women rarely stepped into traditionally male-dominated roles, Shanti decided to break the mold.

With no formal training but an unyielding resolve, Shanti Devi began to learn the basics of truck mechanics by observing the men at work. Her keen interest and quick learning skills soon caught the attention of young, Vishnu. Recognizing her potential, Vishnu sought Shanti Devi's permission to enter her picture (see below) to an international photo contest led by the World Association of Christian Communication (WACC) focused on 'Portraying gender' and 'busting gender stereotypes.' Shanti Devi agreed. Vishnu worked under the guidance of his photography mentor, Mahesh Nair, to capture numerous pictures of Shanti Devi at work at her workshop. These were submitted to WACC's global photography contest, which won Vishnu 3rd position among seventeen hundred photo entries worldwide. This shot Vishnu and Shanti Devi to fame.

Award Winning Photo of Shanti Devi (Credited to Vishnu)

Empowerment Through Skill Development

Inspired by Shanti's story, Vishnu saw an opportunity to amplify her impact. He believed that Shanti's journey could inspire other women and marginalized individuals in the community to pursue bold, non-traditional roles. Vishnu collaborated with local NGOs, media, and the Center for Human Progress to set up discussions for women in Sanjay Gandhi Transport Nagar. With the engagement of the press and the proliferation of information thanks to media and the internet, Shanti Devi's story reached international realms within hours.

The advocacy, spearheaded by Shanti Devi and Vishnu, inspired women worldwide. Shanti Devi's hands-on approach and relatable story made her an effective mentor. She shared her experiences, emphasizing the importance of resilience, continuous learning, and self-belief.

Read more here: http://www.thechp.org/press---awards.html

Here is just one of numerous videos and media interviews with Shanti Devi: https://www.youtube.com/watch?v=siN0etP7FMI

Overcoming Challenges

The initiative faced significant resistance initially. Many in the community were skeptical about women working as mechanics, a role traditionally reserved for men. However, Shanti Devi's growing reputation as a competent mechanic and unwavering determination slowly changed perceptions. Vishnu worked tirelessly to gain the community's trust, organizing awareness campaigns and community meetings to highlight the program's benefits.

Shanti Devi's success as a mechanic and mentor began to draw more women to the fold. Slowly but surely, the number of women entering the field of gender advocates increased. These women, empowered by their newfound skills and confidence, began challenging the status quo, paving the way for future generations.

Women's Empowerment and Gender Advocacy

Building on the success of the gender advocacy program, Vishnu expanded the scope of his community initiatives. He helped establish community-run groups, especially for women focused on sustainable practices and informal cooperatives that provide training and resources to communities, aiming to increase productivity while preserving the environment. The cooperatives also created a sense of ownership and self-reliance among their peers, empowering them to take charge of their future.

One of the cooperatives, led by Shanti Devi and other women, specialized in handmade crafts. This initiative not only provided an additional source of income but also promoted sustainable practices. The cooperative's success attracted attention from nearby communities, inspiring more women to join and replicate the model.

Health and Education Initiatives

Vishnu also focused on health and education initiatives, recognizing the importance of holistic development. He collaborated with local health professionals to set up health camps in Sanjay Gandhi Transport Nagar and nearby areas. These camps provided free medical check-ups, vaccinations, and health education sessions about HIV and Sexually Transmitted Infections (STIs), which were highly prevalent among truck drivers, through entertainment education and awareness events. Special attention was given to the health issues truck drivers and their families faced, addressing problems such as HIV, substance abuse, and STI risk reduction.

Vishnu's Initiative with NACO

Vishnu and the Red Ribbon Express Led by NACO

HIV Risk Reduction Programs at the NACO Event

Through the Center for Human Progress, Vishnu also played a significant role in supporting the National AIDS Control Organization (NACO), the Ministry of Health and Family Welfare's department of AIDS control, with its interventions across India. He was actively involved in initiatives such as NACO's flagship Red Ribbon Express, a mobile HIV and AIDS awareness campaign that traveled to rural and underserved areas. Vishnu's contributions included organizing and educational programs, facilitating testing and counseling services, and promoting awareness about HIV prevention and treatment. His efforts helped extend the reach of NACO's vital work, bringing much-needed support and information to communities that otherwise had limited access to healthcare resources.

Vishnu and His Team Mate, Harun Ahmed Stood Strong in Solidarity for HIV Prevention

In addition to health camps, Vishnu improved educational opportunities for children in the community. He partnered with local groups and NGOs to provide support, technical skills, and career counseling. The aim was to ensure that children, especially girls, had access to quality education and the support needed to pursue their dreams.

Vishnu Trains Children

Shanti Devi played a crucial role in these SHGs, sharing her journey and encouraging other women to pursue their aspirations. Her story of resilience and empowerment became a beacon of hope, demonstrating that overcoming societal barriers and achieving success was possible.

Read more about entertainment education initiatives led by and for communities through Vishnu's facilitation and leadership at the Center for Human Progress.

CONDOLYMPICS

Condolympics: http://www.thechp.org/projects-3.html. **International Entertainment Education Conference (EE5):** http://www.thechp.org/projects-2.html. **Red Ribbon on the Road:** http://www.thechp.org/red-ribbon-on-the-road.html

Vishnu and His Co-Facilitators After a Workshop in Mumbai, India

Creating a Network of Support

Vishnu understood that sustainable change required a strong support network. He facilitated the formation of informal community, self-help groups (SHGs) for women and vulnerable groups (e.g., LGBTQI communities), where they could share their experiences, support each other, and collectively address their challenges. Many of these groups became community-based organization, formal and informal networks, and platforms for women and marginalized communities to discuss various issues, from domestic violence to financial literacy, and find solutions together.

Empowering Women: Vishnu's Role in Community Transformation

During his tireless efforts to empower communities, Vishnu played a key role in supporting women's groups, including the *Mahila Panchayat* and *Mahila Ayog*, India (*Mahila* is a Hindi word, which means women). Collaborating closely with peer leaders from the community, such as the dedicated and inspirational young women leaders like Meera, he helped establish support systems for women in need. These initiatives provided vital resources, advocacy, and training, enabling women to gain confidence and self-reliance. Vishnu's work with these groups not only addressed immediate needs but also fostered long-term empowerment and resilience among the women, significantly improving their lives and standing in the community.

Vishnu with Village Women Near Sanjay Gandhi Transport Nagar

Vishnu and Meera, along with other community leaders, worked diligently to establish comprehensive support systems for women in need. These initiatives provided essential resources, advocacy, and training programs designed to help women gain confidence and self-reliance. Vishnu's efforts went beyond addressing immediate needs; he aimed to foster long-term empowerment and resilience among the women, significantly improving their lives and standing in the community. Collaborating with peer leaders like the dedicated Meera, they helped establish support systems that provided these women with essential resources, advocacy, and a safe space to rebuild their lives. Their efforts not only addressed women's immediate needs but also empowered them to regain their dignity and self-reliance, fostering a sense of community and resilience.

A major focus of their work was assisting women who had been violated or ostracized by their families due to the stigma of being HIV-positive. This group of women faced severe social and economic challenges, and Vishnu, with Meera's collaboration, provided them with crucial support systems. They created safe spaces where these women could rebuild their lives, offering essential resources, advocacy, and emotional support.

Their efforts were multifaceted, addressing both the urgent and long-term needs of these women. They organized workshops on health and hygiene, provided training in vocational skills, and offered legal aid to ensure that these women could stand up for their rights. By helping them regain their dignity and self-reliance, Vishnu and his team fostered a sense of community and resilience.

The impact of Vishnu's work was profound. Women who had once felt isolated and powerless began to find their voices and assert their rights. The initiatives he helped establish not only provided immediate relief but also laid the groundwork for sustainable change. Through his dedication and compassion, Vishnu empowered these women to transform their lives, creating a ripple effect that uplifted the entire community.

Vishnu's role in these initiatives exemplifies his broader mission: to create in-clusive, supportive environments where every individual has the opportunity to thrive. His work with the *Mahila Panchayat* and *Mahila Ayog* stands as a testament to his unwavering commitment to social justice and empowerment, showcasing the powerful impact of community-driven change. Visit Mahila Panchayat at: http://www.abhivyaktifoundation.in/portfolio/mhl/index.ht ml

Advocacy and Policy Change

Vishnu's work in community empowerment extended beyond grassroots initiatives. He actively engaged in community and policy advocacy, working with local stakeholders and government officials to create a more supportive environment for women, vulnerable, and marginalized communities. He lobbied for better working conditions for truck drivers, gender equality in the workforce, and increased investment in education and health. Vishnu integrated these principles and philosophy into his work with the POP Movement, focusing on empowering individuals to take charge of their future.

Vishnu at a Red Ribbon on the Road Workhshop

Vishnu Training at a Red Ribbon on the Road Workshop Sponsored by IKEA

Vishnu at an IKEA Sponsored Workshop with Truck Drivers

Condolympics Activities at an IKEA Workshop

Vishnu Preparing for a Magnet Theater Performance

Vishnu Conducting an Ice Breaker at an IKEA Workshop

Vishnu with His Team and Officials at an IKEA Workshop

His advocacy initiatives led by significant documentation efforts using creative formats including photography, film, and creative art helped showcase issues to wide audiences, while mainstreaming issues. He displayed his work online and offline through community-led events, including many at Sanjay Gandhi Transport Nagar.He advocated for stricter regulations on working hours and safety standards for truck drivers through collaboration with partners including IKEA(read more about the project here: http://www.thechp.org/red-ribbon-on-the-road.html) through the Center for Human Progress. Inspired by the successes of Shanti Devi and Meera, the government also introduced incentives for companies to hire women in traditionally male-dominated roles.

Rising Influence

Vishnu's work with the POP Movement soon garnered international attention. He was invited to join global forums, including the World Sustainable Development Forum, the International Conference & POP Festival, the Conference of the Parties (COP28), and other local and global events, to lead entertainment education initiatives, storytelling, and advocacy through his rapidly developing multimedia work, which now included the use of Artificial Intelligence (AI), design programs, and sophisticated filming and postproduction programs. He joined several international platforms to strengthen advocacy for urgent climate action and health equity. His technical skills in multimedia and participatory communications were powerful, filled with passion and personal anecdotes that resonated with audiences.

Checkout the links below:

Vishnu's film **Wheels of Revolution** was entered to the Human Rights Watch International Film Festival and was selected for screening on a New York television network in 2010.

Expressions grf Empowerment: Truckers Armed with Cameras Share Vision
Read more at http://www.thechp.org/press---awards.html

Through these platforms, Vishnu developed films highlighting the struggles of marginalized communities, particularly those he had grown up with. He emphasized personal stories to empower youth and giving them the tools to effect change. His pictures, films, visuals worth more than a thousand words, inspired many to join the cause, and the POP Movement saw a surge in young activists ready to make a difference.

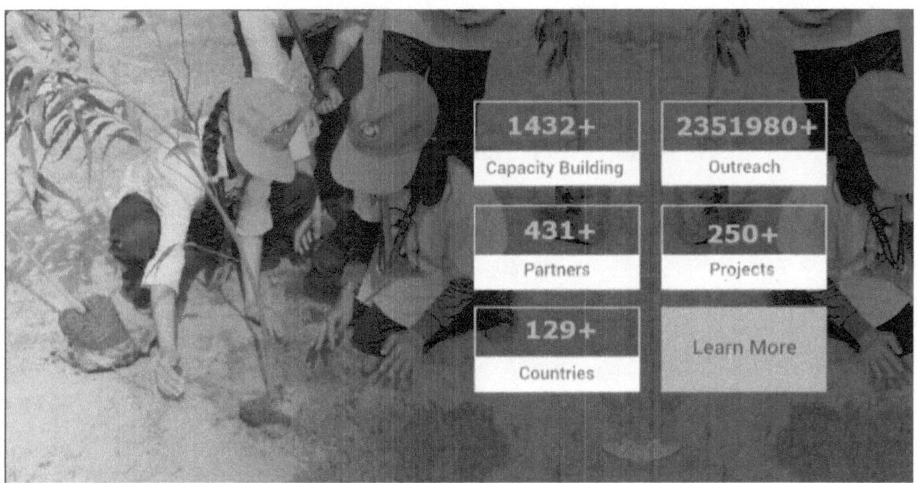

Learn More at www.thepopmovement.org

Despite his growing influence, Vishnu never forgot his roots. He launched several initiatives to support truck drivers and their families back in Sanjay Gandhi Transport Nagar, where he continues to live, even as he frequently travels internationally. He collaborates with local community-based organizations and NGOs to set up health camps, provide educational opportunities, and advocate for better working conditions. These efforts brought tangible improvements to the lives of the drivers and their families.

Self-Care with the Most Vulnerable and Marginalized Communities

In addition to his extensive work in community empowerment and climate action, Vishnu also made significant contributions to the field of self-care interventions for health. Recognizing the importance of self-care in improving public health outcomes, Vishnu visually documented global self-care interventions through his role with the Center for Human Progress.

Leading Film and Photography

Vishnu took on a pivotal role in this project, leading and managing all the film and photography efforts in addition to being a co-facilitator and trainer at the community workshops. His expertise in visual storytelling allowed him to create compelling visuals that effectively communicated the importance of self-care practices. These visuals were not only instrumental in the project's outreach but also gained widespread recognition.

Global Recognition

The impact of Vishnu's work extended far beyond local communities. His visuals on self-care were widely published by the World Health Organization (WHO) in Geneva, bringing global attention to the project. Through his creative efforts, Vishnu helped raise awareness about self-care interventions and their role in enhancing health outcomes worldwide.

By combining his technical skills with his passion for public health, Vishnu continues to inspire and drive change, making a lasting impact on both a local and global scale.

Visit Vishnu's work on self-care here: http://www.thechp.org/self-care-interventions-for-health.html

Self-Care with Truck Drivers at Sanjay Gandhi Transport Nagar

Vishnu and His Team After a Self-Care Workshop in Mexico

Vishnu at Self-Care Workshop with Health Practitioners

Vishnu with His Self-Care Team

Vishnu at Self-Care Workshop in Hyderabad, India

Vishnu at a Self-Care Workshop with Fashion Models

Vishnu with 'Toda' Indigenous Women in Tamil Nadu, India

Vishnu and His Peers After a Self-Care Workshop in Cancun, Mexico

Rising Leadership

As Vishnu's influence grew, so did his responsibilities. He took on more significant roles within the POP Movement, leading the documentation of large-scale projects and training his less experienced peers and youth in participatory, peer-led communication and research methodologies.

Vishnu in Sargassum, Cancun, Mexico

His work took him to various countries, including Mexico and Dubai, where he continued to champion the causes of climate action and health advocacy. He continues to lead community work with the most vulnerable adolescents and youth on self-care globally; and climate action initiatives focused on sargassum (an invasive seaweed) and the impacts of climate on human health in Mexico and elsewhere.

On the Way to Cancun, Mexico

Some of Vishnu's most ambitious projects were to lead community work with the most vulnerable adolescents, youth, and communities on self-care globally; and climate action research focused on sargassum and interactions between ocean and human health in Mexico. He believes that empowering young people is crucial for sustainable change. Through workshops, training programs, and international conferences, he has brought together young activists from around the world, fostering a sense of solidarity and shared purpose.

Camera in Cancun, Mexico

Vishnu with His Research Team in Cancun, Mexico

With his initiative, the POP Movement launched several innovative programs, including a youth-led school training initiative to reach urban students to campaign for renewable energy, tree plantation, water sanitation, and green schools in urban and rural areas. Vishnu's leadership style—collaborative, inclusive, and driven by a deep sense of empathy—earned him admiration and respect from his peers.

Vishnu and Members of the POP Movement Conduct Research on Sargassum, Cancun, Mexico

Vishnu with the POP Family in Cancun, Mexico

Vishnu's Life is Never All Work and No Play, Cancun, Mexico

Challenges and Triumphs

Vishnu's journey was not without its share of heart-wrenching turmoil and hard-won triumphs. Amidst his growing influence and achievements, life threw several formidable challenges his way, testing his resilience and fortitude.

The Loss of Loved Ones

Sanjay Gandhi Transport Nagar was more than just a home to Vishnu; it was the crucible where his character was forged. His father, Ramesh Gupta, a skilled farmer, and his uncle and aunt, who raised him like a son, were his pillars of strength. Their sudden and untimely deaths, in rapid sequence, left a void in Vishnu's heart, shaking the very foundation of his life. The grief was profound, but it also strengthened his resolve to honor their legacy through his work.

Separation During the Pandemic

Amidst the global pandemic, Vishnu faced a wave of hardship that tested his resolve both personally and professionally. Having recently married a lovely young lady from his village, their union was filled with promise and joy. However, their happiness was short-lived. As the pandemic spread, lockdowns were enforced, and Vishnu found himself separated from his new bride, stranded in Delhi while she was confined to their village. The year of separation was agonizing, marked by uncertainty and longing. Despite the distance and the pandemic's relentless grip, their love and commitment to each other remained unwavering.

Vishnu's professional life was equally demanding during this period. Deeply committed to his work and maintaining an extraordinary level of professionalism, he traveled to Durango, Mexico, the day after his wedding, to help administer the World Sustainable Development Forum 2020. This international conference, attended by over 2,000 heads of state, scientists, and youth from around the world, was a significant event in the sustainability sector. Tragically, just days before the forum, his Chief Mentor and father figure, the late Dr. R.K. Pachauri, leader and President of the World Sustainable Development Forum, passed away (see www.worldsdf.org).

In the months leading up to Dr. Pachauri's passing, Vishnu had been by his side, nursing him alongside the Pachauri family. He often spent days and nights in the hospital, providing not just physical care but also emotional support. They talked about sports, climate change, urgent work that needed to be done, and life in general, often in an effort to distract from Dr. Pachauri's ailing health. These moments deepened Vishnu's bond with his mentor, making the loss even more profound.

Despite the personal loss and the immense pressure, Vishnu did not falter in his commitment to Dr. R.K. Pachauri's legacy and his son, Senior Mentor Dr. Ash Pachauri, who was more than a friend to him. He played a pivotal role in ensuring the forum's success, honoring Dr. Pachauri's memory with a highly successful event that garnered global attention. Visit https://worldsdf.org/events/durango-mexico-march-2020/.

The day Vishnu returned to India, a nationwide lockdown was declared, leaving him stranded in Delhi while his wife remained in their village. Their separation continued for nearly a year, adding to the emotional and psychological toll of the pandemic. Yet, through these personal and professional trials, Vishnu's dedication and resilience shone through, reinforcing his commitment to his mission and the people he aimed to serve.

During the pandemic, Vishnu moved into the Pachauri home for nearly a year, becoming an integral part of the family. Living with the Pachauri family during the pandemic, Vishnu's role extended beyond that of a friend or colleague. He was a son to Dr. Saroj Pachauri, offering her the companionship and support she needed after the loss of her husband. His bond with Dr. Ash Pachauri deepened, evolving into a brotherhood forged through shared grief, pain, and mutual respect. Vishnu also took care of Dr. Ash Pachauri's sisters, treating them with the same love and care he would offer his own family.

Vishnu was cared for and also provided care in return during the pandemic. This period of close-knit support and mutual reliance showcased the profound strength of their relationships, fostering an enduring bond built on love, trust, and shared experiences. In this period, he also strengthened his resolve to dedicate his life's work to his beloved, Late Chief Mentor and the Pachauri family.

Vishnu's unwavering resolve during this tumultuous time exemplifies his strength of character and deep sense of duty. His ability to navigate these challenges with grace and determination continues to inspire those around him, showcasing the profound impact of his work and his enduring commitment to making a difference. Despite the emotional demands of his personal life, Vishnu balanced these responsibilities with his professional commitments. He remained deeply involved in the POP Movement, driving forward initiatives that empowered communities and promoted sustainable practices. His ability to manage these dual roles with grace and determination was a testament to his resilience and dedication.

Vishnu in Durango, Mexico with His Mentors and the Government of Durango, Mexico

Vishnu with, the then, Governor of Durango, Mexico

World Sustainable Development Forum, 2020, Durango, Mexico

Vishnu with Former Prime Minister of Japan, Dr. Yukio Hatoyama in Durango, Mexico

Watch the World Sustainable Development Forum Here:
https://www.youtube.com/watch?v=RoIMVHqszco&t=2s or Visit
https://worldsdf.org/events/durango-mexico-march-2020/

Climate Change Devastation

As if the separation from his wife wasn't enough, climate change dealt another blow. A severe weather event destroyed the house Vishnu lived in in Sanjay Gandhi Transport Nagar. Stranded and separated from his wife, Vishnu faced what seemed like insurmountable odds. Yet, he refused to succumb to despair. Drawing strength from his past experiences and his unwavering belief in his mission, he pressed on, determined to rebuild his life and continue his work.

Tireless Effort During the Pandemic

Undeterred by his own challenges, Vishnu worked tirelessly and selflessly with community leaders like Shanti Devi and Meera to support the most vulnerable during the pandemic. They organized initiatives in slum areas around Sanjay Gandhi Transport Nagar (e.g., Sanjay Colony, Samaypur on the border of Delhi and its neighboring state Haryana) to feed the homeless, economically challenged, and those suffering due to the lockdowns. Their efforts ensured that thousands of meals were distributed, providing not only sustenance but also hope and a sense of community to those in dire need. Vishnu's dedication during this challenging time exemplified his unwavering commitment to helping others, regardless of the circumstances.

A New Beginning

Today, Vishnu's perseverance has paid off. He is reunited with his wife, and they now live together in Delhi, in their own home. Vishnu's newly refurbished house is not just a symbol of his triumph over adversity but also a testament to his commitment to sustainability. He bought and renovated his property to withstand severe climate events, ensuring that his family are better protected against future threats.

Vishnu is now a proud homeowner and a new father to his nine-month-old son. The joy of parenthood has brought a new dimension to his life, filling it with hope and purpose. His household is bustling with life, as he supports not only his wife and son but also his mother, brother, and his brother's family, all living together under one roof.

Sustaining His Family and Legacy

The challenges Vishnu faced have only solidified his resolve to support and uplift those around him. His home has become a sanctuary, a place where his family can thrive and where the principles of sustainability and resilience are lived out daily. He continues to support his mother, who has been a source of strength throughout his journey, and his brother, who is now working at Sanjay Gandhi Transport Nagar.

Vishnu's wife is now supporting him in his pursuit of community empowerment by helping over 200 women obtain clean cooking gas through a government program, *Pradhan Mantri Ujjwala Yojana 2.0*. Recognizing that many of these women are illiterate, technologically challenged, and unable to access this digital service, Vishnu mobilized his family to support the women in his community. Together, they assist young women in availing government programs for clean cooking gas and utilities. Their collective efforts ensure that even the most vulnerable can benefit from these crucial services, promoting health, safety, and economic empowerment within the community. He utilizes every opportunity to interact with the community to educate them about health, equity, and sustainability.

A Story of Resilience

In addition to personal tribulations, Vishnu faced numerous uphill battles at work. Engaging with a global movement required navigating complex cultural differences, building language skills (including spoken English), learning to write, email, and document, managing diverse relationships, and adopting technology (from simple applications like Word to searching the World Wide Web). Vishnu has mastered these skills and many more, now, being adept in AI applications, sophisticated multimedia and visual editing tools including Canva and Photoshop among many others. Initially, though, progress seemed slow, and setbacks threatened to derail his efforts. However, Vishnu's unwavering commitment and resilience kept him moving forward.

One of the significant challenges he faced was applying participatory and inclusive approaches when speaking with communities other than his own. Vishnu had to engage with delicate situations and sensitivities (e.g., working among communities, such as female and transgender sex workers, which he was initially unfamiliar with), while balancing advocacy and training with empathy and compassion. His ability to articulate the long-term benefits of community empowerment, health promotion, and sustainable practices eventually won over many skeptics, though it was often a hard-fought battle.

Vishnu Mastering the Use of Computers and Computer Applications

Vishnu Mastering Computer Technology

Vishnu is Exposed to Varied Cultural Experiences

Vishnu at the COP28, Dubai, United Arab Emirates

Despite these hurdles, Vishu's work brought about meaningful change. The initiatives he led improved the quality of life for countless individuals and contributed to a growing global awareness of environmental and health issues as well as the intersection between the two. His impact was felt not just at the direct community-level through changes and improved health education and outcomes, but also in the growing number of young people inspired to take action.

Vishnu at School Educational Programs to Protect Our Planet

A Beacon of Hope

Vishnu's personal and professional stories of turmoil and triumphs is a powerful reminder of the resilience of the human spirit. His ability to overcome personal loss, endure separation, and rebuild his life in the face of climate disasters speaks volumes about his character. It also underscores the importance of community and family support in navigating life's challenges.

Today, Vishnu stands as a beacon of hope and inspiration. His journey from the bustling lanes of Sanjay Gandhi Transport Nagar to becoming a global leader in climate action and community empowerment is a testament to the power of perseverance, love, and an unyielding commitment to making the world a better place. His life, marked by profound personal losses and triumphant victories, continues to inspire those who face their own battles, proving that with determination and support, one can overcome any adversity.

Full Circle

Vishnu's journey comes full circle every day when he returns to Sanjay Gandhi Transport Nagar (where he still lives) as a respected leader and advocate. The community that shaped him greets him with pride and admiration. His initiatives have already improved their lives significantly, and his continued commitment promises even more positive changes as he continues to work with the most vulnerable and marginalized people in his surroundings.

Vishnu's resolve to Work toward the Sustainable Development Goals is Strong

Vishnu's story inspires people worldwide, not just truck drivers and their families. His rise from a helper at a truck stop to a global leader demonstrates the power of perseverance, education, and compassion. He has shown that one person, driven by a desire to make a difference, can change the world.

With a firm foundation established, Vishnu has begun envisioning even broader goals for the POP Movement. He aims to integrate climate action with economic initiative, creating sustainable livelihoods while protecting the environment. His vision is to make environmental sustainability a core part of community growth and development.

He has initiated collaborations with diverse communities and partners to develop and implement projects that combine environmental conservation with economic empowerment. These projects include sustainable agriculture programs, eco-tourism initiatives, and greening initiatives. Vishnu believes that by aligning economic incentives with environmental goals, lasting change could be achieved.

Legacy of Hope

Today, Vishnu continues to propel youth in the POP Movement with unwavering dedication. His journey is a testament to the impact one individual can have when they refuse to be defined by their circumstances. He has inspired countless others to take up the mantle of climate action and health advocacy through his work.

Vishnu's legacy is one of hope and empowerment. He has proven that even the most marginalized voices can rise to effect meaningful change. As he continues to travel around India and the world, attend and organize events, launch new initiatives, and mentor young leaders, his story remains a beacon of inspiration for all who strive to make a difference.

Continuing the Journey

As Vishnu looks to the future, he remains steadfast in his commitment to creating a more sustainable and equitable world. He continues to innovate, finding new ways to engage communities and inspire action. His journey is far from over; he knows the road ahead will be filled with challenges and opportunities.

Balancing the demands of his personal life with his professional commitments, Vishnu's resolve is unwavering. He continues to honor his commitments to the POP Movement while maintaining the deep, familial bonds with the Pachauri family. They are not just his friends; they are his family in every sense, providing him with a foundation of love and support that fuels his drive to make a difference.

A Legacy of Hope and Empowerment

Vishnu's story powerfully reminds us that no matter where you come from or what obstacles you face, it is possible to make a profound impact on the world. His life is a testament to the power of perseverance, education, and compassion. Vishnu's grit and determination continue to build a legacy of hope, empowerment, and lasting change through his work with the POP Movement and beyond.

As he navigates the complexities of his dual roles, Vishnu remains an inspiration to all who know him. His journey exemplifies the impact one individual can have when driven by a deep sense of purpose and a commitment to service. Through his tireless efforts, Vishnu is not only changing lives today but also laying the groundwork for a brighter, more sustainable future for generations to come.

A Message of Gratitude

D ear Readers,

Thank you for taking the time to read my story. Your support means the world to me and to all those who have been part of this journey. As you have seen, my life has been a testament to the power of resilience, community, and the unwavering belief that we can all make a difference.

I humbly request you to leave an honest review of this book. Your feedback is incredibly valuable and can help spread our message to a wider audience. By sharing your thoughts and experiences, you will play a crucial role in inspiring more young leaders and supporting vulnerable communities like mine. Every review not only helps this book reach more readers but also strengthens our collective effort to drive positive change. Your words can encourage others to join the cause, support sustainable initiatives, and empower those in need.

Thank you for being a part of this journey. Together, we can continue to build a more equitable and sustainable world.

With gratitude,

Vishnu

I am now a Youth Mentor at the POP Movement (manish@thepopmovement.org). Read more about me here https://thepopmovement.org/team/manish-gupta/

In addition to various media articles, my story has been written about in the book entitled "Sexual and Reproductive Health and Rights in India: Self-care for Universal Health Coverage (SpringerBriefs in Public Health) documented by Dr Rashmi Pachauri Rajan available here: https://link.springer.com/chapter/10.1007/978-981-16-4578-5_5

I am a Master Trainer

a. Participatory dialogue-based communication, including Interpersonal Communication and Magnet Theater.

b. Photography (trained by Nat Geo photographer, Mahesh Nair) for community empowerment.

c. Documentary film making (self-trained and trained by Vasvya Mahila Mandli or VMM, India) for community advocacy.

3. My Achievements Include the Following

a. Award winning photography (by the World Academy of Christian Communication or WACC). Checkout my award winning photo of 2009 here. Visit http://www.thechp.org/

b. The Toronto Film Festival nominated my film, "Wheels of Revolution". Visit http://www.thechp.org/ to learn more.

c. My film **Wheels of Revolution** about the life and issues of truck drivers was submitted to the Human Rights Watch International Film Festival and was selected for screening by a New York television network in 2010. Visit http://www.thechp.org/

4. I am a Trained Documentary Film Maker

I have developed several documentary films and contributed to one photo essay publication which was showcased at an Indian national sex worker festival in Mysore in 2009. The publication was about HIV positive (male/female and transgender) sex workers. Check it out the Positive Habba here. http://www.thechp.org/films---publications.html

5. This is My Training and Teaching Experience

My language, computer applications, and creative design skills are self-taught. I put myself through college qualifying in a bachelor's in social work from India Gandhi National Open University, India in 2019.

Through my work, I have conducted numerous training programs globally and taught along with my Mentor, Dr. Ash Pachauri through the Center for Human Progress and the POP Movement, including at the International Institute of Health Management Research.

I intend to continue building community leadership and empowerment through my endeavors in the fields of environment, public health, and technology.